No Nonsense
Maths

6-7 years

Central pull-out pages

Parents' notes   A1
Answers   A2-4

Contents

www.bondlearning.co.uk

Read and write numbers to 100

100 = = 10 tens

46 = = 4 tens 6 units

1. Colour in the correct number of tens and units.

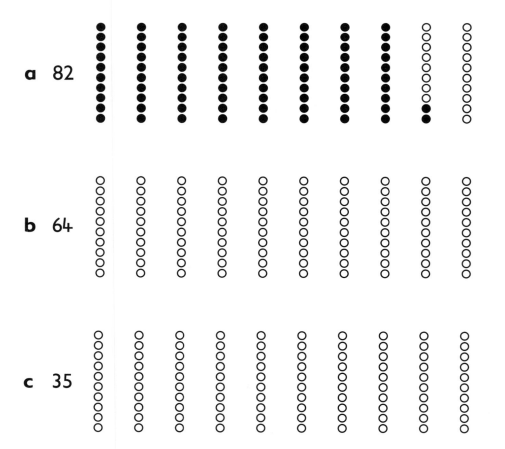

a   82

b   64

c   35

2. **How many? Write the number.**

a

= 7 tens 2 units = _____

b

= 4 tens 5 units = _____

c

= 5 tens 8 units = _____

3. **a** 53 = _____ tens _____ units   **b** 28 = _____ tens _____ units

c 97 = _____ tens _____ units   **d** 36 = _____ tens _____ units

How did I do?			

Total

/9

More practice? Go to **www**

Challenge yourself

Write these numbers in words.

a 53 _____

b 49 _____

c 81 _____

Now write these numbers in figures.

d twenty-six _____   **e** ninety-three _____

f fifty-five _____   **g** eighty-six _____

3

Order and count numbers to 100

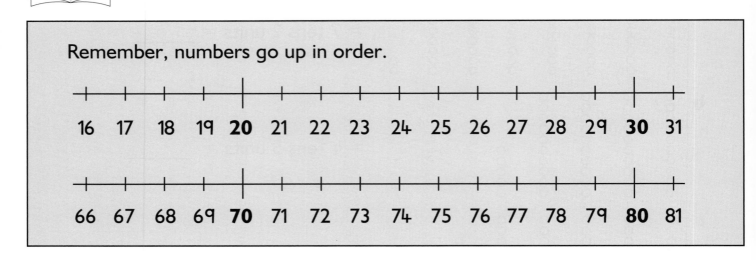

Remember, numbers go up in order.

16 17 18 19 **20** 21 22 23 24 25 26 27 28 29 **30** 31

66 67 68 69 **70** 71 72 73 74 75 76 77 78 79 **80** 81

1. Join the dots to make shapes. Start on ✕ each time.

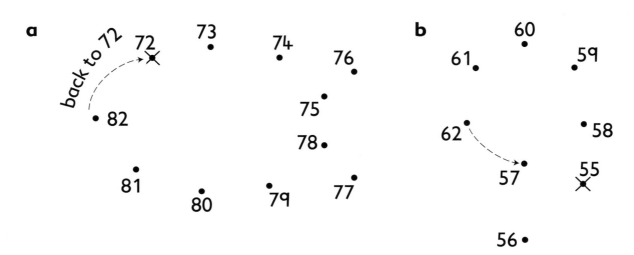

a

back to 72   72 ✕   73   74   76
• 82   75   78•
81   80   79   77   56•
57   55 ✕

b

60   61•   59•
62   58•
57   55 ✕
56•

c

33•
43 •----→✕ 32   34   •35
42 •   • 36
41   40   38   37
39

d

19• 20 •21
18•   • 22
✕ 17 23
40• 37   •27   •24
39 38 •36 28•   26 25
•32
35•   29
34• 33   31 •30

2. Fill in the missing numbers.

a 61   62   63   ☐   65   66

b 47   ☐   49   50   51   52

c 83   84   85   86   ☐   88

d 17   18   ☐   20   ☐   22

e 26   27   28   ☐   30   ☐

3. Which number is smaller?

a 68 or 45? _____   b 21 or 33? _____

c 83 or 73? _____   d 12 or 11? _____

e 38 or 29? _____   f 46 or 64? _____

4. Which number is bigger?

a 28 or 18? _____   b 22 or 12? _____

c 57 or 55? _____   d 69 or 77? _____

e 32 or 17? _____   f 51 or 55? _____

How did I do?

Total ☐/21

More practice? Go to www

Challenge yourself

Write a number that comes between the two numbers.

a 21 _24_ 26   b 38 _____ 41

c 19 _____ 24   d 29 _____ 33

e 31 _____ 33   f 68 _____ 72

g 97 _____ 99   h 77 _____ 82

Tens and units

Look at the number **43**.

		T		U

43 is **4 tens** and **3 units**

1. Fill in the gaps.

a 63 = = _____ tens _____ units

b 28 = = _____ tens _____ units

c 51 = = _____ tens _____ unit

2. How many tens and units?

a 23 = _2_ tens _3_ units **b** 48 = ____ tens ____ units

c 57 = ____ tens ____ units **d** 89 = ____ tens ____ units

3. **Join with a line the number in figures with the number in words.**

47   six tens and five units

72   nine tens and three units

65   two tens and two units

22   five tens and nine units

93   four tens and seven units

59   seven tens and two units

How did I do?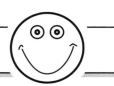

Total
[/12]

More practice? Go to www

Challenge yourself

Each empty box needs a number to make the number sentences correct.

a 99 = [ ] + 9   **b** 53 = 50 + [ ]

c [ ] = 10 + 7   **d** 86 = 80 + [ ]

e 37 = [ ] + 7   **f** [ ] = 40 + 2

Odd and even numbers

If a number can be split exactly in two it is an **even** number.

14 =

7   7   = even

If a number cannot be split exactly in two it is an **odd** number.

15 =

7   8   = odd

1.   **Are these numbers odd or even?**

   a   6 = 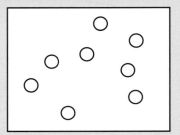   =   ___even___

          3   3

   b   11 =

          5   6   =   _____

   c   17 =

          8   9   =   _____

2. Odd or even?

a 15 = [circles] [circles] = *odd*

  _7_ _8_

b 16 = [ ] [ ] = _____

  ___ ___

c 21 = [ ] [ ] = _____

  ___ ___

d 28 = [ ] [ ] = _____

  ___ ___

e 25 = [ ] [ ] = _____

  ___ ___

How did I do?			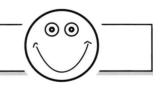	Total

Total /6

More practice? Go to

More practice? Go to www

Challenge yourself

Colour the

a odd numbers blue.   **b** even numbers yellow.

9	10	11	12	13	14	15	16	17	18	19	20	21	22	23	24	25	26	27	28

Subtraction 1

Do you remember how to subtract?

$$15 - 6 = 9$$

1. **Use the apples to write a number sentence.**

a  ____13____ – ____6____ = _____

b  _____ – _____ = _____

c  _____ – _____ = _____

d  _____ – _____ = _____

e  _____ – _____ = _____

2. Now try these. Use pictures if it helps.

    a 12 – 5 = _____

    b 17 – 7 = _____

    c 20 – 8 = _____

    d 14 – 5 = _____

3. Find the answers.

    a How many less is 7 than 8? _____

    b Take 50 from 70. _____

    c How many must I take from 20 to leave 12? _____

    d How many less is 9 than 19? _____

4. Take 0 from each of these numbers.

    a 14 _____   **b** 23 _____   **c** 19 _____   **d** 26 _____   **e** 15 _____

What do you notice about the answer each time?

_____

_____ ☹ _____ 😐 _____ 🙂 _____

| How did I do? |

Total
/18

More practice? Go to www

Challenge yourself

Put the correct missing numbers in the boxes.

    a 12p – ▢ p = 6p

    b 20p – 8p = ▢ p

    c ▢ p – 9p = 7p

    d 17p – ▢ p = 11p

    e 26p – 10p = ▢ p

    f ▢ p – 5p = 18p

Add and subtract 9

There is an easy way to **add 9** to a number. $7 + 9 = ?$

Instead of adding 9, **add 10 then subtract 1!**

$7 + 10 = 17$ then $17 - 1 = 16$ $7 + 9 = 16$

1. **First add 10 to each of these numbers, then subtract 1.**

a $9 + 10 - 1 =$ _____   b $13 + 10 - 1 =$ _____

c $22 + 10 - 1 =$ _____   d $27 + 10 - 1 =$ _____

e $16 + 10 - 1 =$ _____   f $4 + 10 - 1 =$ _____

2. **Answer these number sentences.**
Use the box to make notes if you need to.

a $14 + 9 =$ _23_

b $17 + 9 =$ _____

c $34 + 9 =$ _____

d $22 + 9 =$ _____

e $76 + 9 =$ _____

f $59 + 9 =$ _____

g $81 + 9 =$ _____

$14 + 10 - 1 = 23$

There is also an easy way to **subtract 9** from a number. $12 - 9 = ?$

Instead of subtracting 9, **subtract 10 then add 1!**

$12 - 10 = 2$ then $2 + 1 = 3$ $12 - 9 = 3$

3. Answer these number sentences.

Use the box to make notes if you need to.

a 24 – 9 = _15_

b 37 – 9 = _____

c 29 – 9 = _____

d 67 – 9 = _____

e 82 – 9 = _____

f 41 – 9 = _____

g 90 – 9 = _____

24 – 10 + 1 = 15

How did I do?

Total

/18

More practice? Go to www

Challenge yourself

Look carefully at these number sentences.
Add the missing signs to make each one correct.

a 25 [+] 9   is the same as   25 [+] 10 [–] 1 = 34

b 57 [ ] 9   is the same as   57 [ ] 10 [ ] 1 = 66

c 45 [ ] 9   is the same as   45 [ ] 10 [ ] 1 = 36

d 18 [ ] 9   is the same as   18 [ ] 10 [ ] 1 = 9

e 79 [ ] 9   is the same as   79 [ ] 10 [ ] 1 = 88

f 54 [ ] 9   is the same as   54 [ ] 10 [ ] 1 = 45

10 times table

2 lots of 10 is 20 | + | = 20

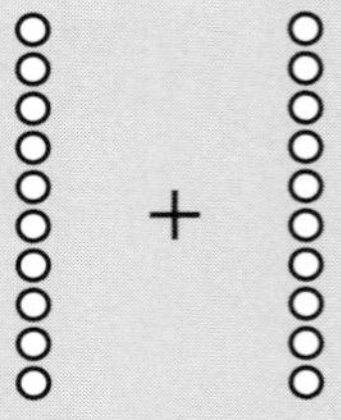

10   10

2 × 10   = 20

> **QUICK TIP!**
> **x** means '**lots of**'
> or '**multiply**'

1.

a   5 × 10 =   = $\underline{50}$

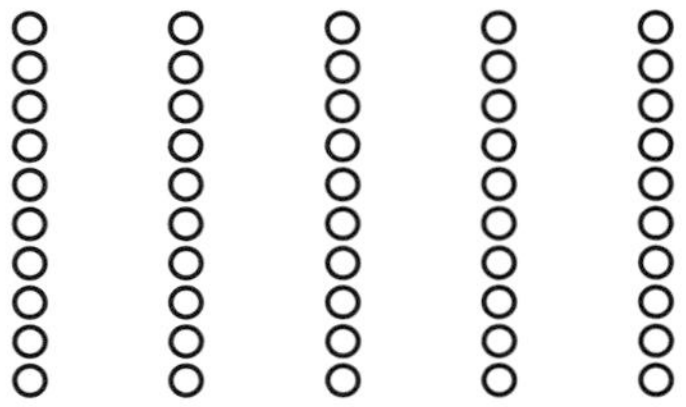

b   3 × 10 =   = ____

c   7 × 10 =   = ____

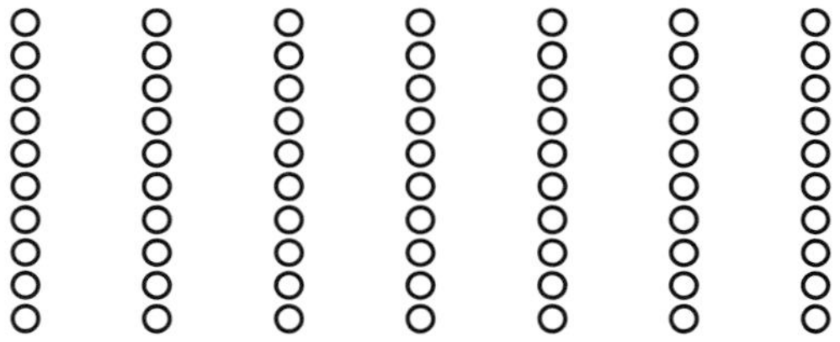

d   4 × 10 =   = ____

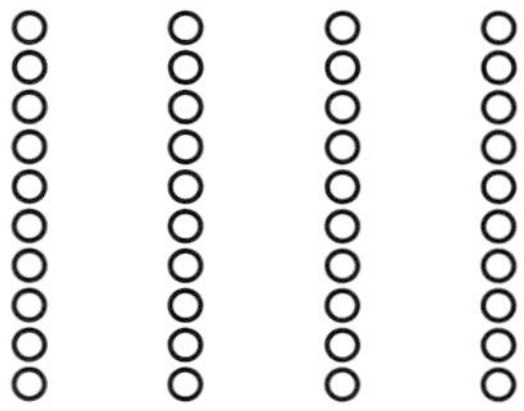

e   1 × 10 =   = ____

2.

$1 \times 10 =$ _____ $6 \times 10 =$ _____

$2 \times 10 =$ _____ $7 \times 10 =$ _____

$3 \times 10 =$ _____ $8 \times 10 =$ _____

$4 \times 10 =$ _____ $9 \times 10 =$ _____

$5 \times 10 =$ _____ $10 \times 10 =$ _____

3. Fill in the gaps.

a $6 \times 10 = \boxed{}$ **b** $8 \times 10 = \boxed{}$ **c** $\boxed{} \times 10 = 30$

d $\boxed{} \times 10 = 50$ **e** $1 \times \boxed{} = 10$ **f** $2 \times \boxed{} = 20$

4. Finish these 10 times table number sequences.

a

10	20		40		60		80	

b

10		30				70	80	90

How did I do? _____ _____ _____  _____

Total
$\boxed{/22}$

More practice? Go to

Challenge yourself

Find the answer!

a Multiply 10 by 6. _____

b What are four tens? _____

c Gaby is given 3 bags of sweets. Each bag has 10 sweets.
How many sweets is she given altogether? _____

Measuring in centimetres and metres

You will need a ruler.

Sometimes we measure length using **metres** and sometimes we use **centimetres**.

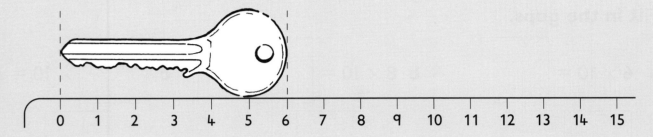

This key is **6 centimetres** long.

We can write centimetres as **cm**.

1. **Measure these pencils using a ruler. Look carefully at the first one.**

a 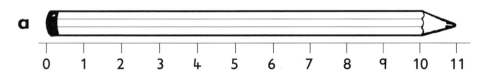   = _____11_____ cm

b   = _____ cm

c   = _____ cm

d   = _____ cm

e   = _____ cm

f   = _____ cm

100 centimetres (cm) = 1 metre (m)

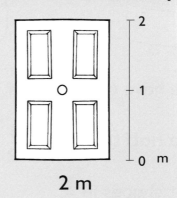

To measure big objects like a door or a car we use **metres (m)**.

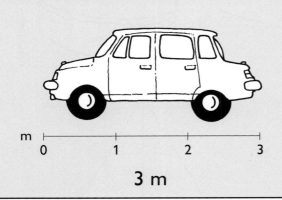

3 m

2 m

2. **Answer these questions.**

   a   How many cm are in 1 m?   _____ cm

   b   Would we use m or cm to measure a garden?   _____

   c   Would we use m or cm to measure a playground?   _____

How did I do?   😞   😐   😊

Total
/8

More practice? Go to **www**

Challenge yourself

Would we use cm or m to measure ...

a   a rubber? _____   b   a book? _____

c   a tree? _____   d   a foot? _____

e   a lorry? _____    f   a pencil? _____

Fractions – a half

Look at this cake. If we cut it into two **equal** parts, it looks like this …

  $\frac{1}{2}$  $\frac{1}{2}$

We say we have cut it in **half**.

We write a **half** like this … $\frac{1}{2}$

We can cut shapes in $\frac{1}{2}$.

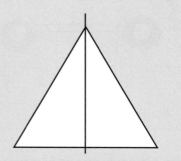

1. **Cut these shapes in half.** Colour $\frac{1}{2}$ of each shape.

a    b 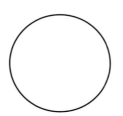   c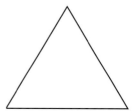

d 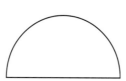   e 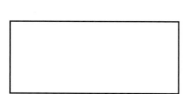   f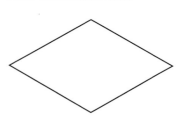

2. **Tick the shapes that have been cut in $\frac{1}{2}$.**

a 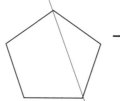 ___   b 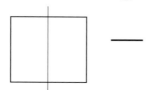 ___   c 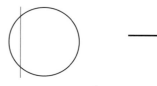 ___

d  ___   e  ___   f 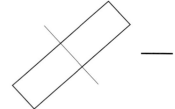 ___

We can work out fractions of a number.

Splitting something in half gives two equal parts.

If we split a number in $\frac{1}{2}$, we do the same.

$\frac{1}{2}$ of 6 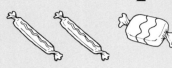 | = 3

3. **Split these groups of sweets in half with a line.**

a

b

c

How did I do?

Total 15

More practice? Go to www

Challenge yourself

Use drawings to help if you need to.

a What is half of 8? _____

b What is half of 14? _____

c What is half of 12? _____

d What is half of 18? _____

e What is half of 6? _____

f What is half of 20? _____

a

How am I doing?

1. **a** 67 = _____ tens _____ units

   b 29 = _____ tens _____ units

   c 36 = _____ tens _____ units

   d 42 = _____ tens _____ units

2. **Fill in the missing numbers.**

   a 28   29   30   [   ]   32   33   [   ]

   b 71   72   [   ]   74   [   ]   76   77

3. **Which number is the same as ...**

   a three tens and three units? _____

   b eight tens and seven units? _____

4. **Odd or even? Try to split the numbers in half.**
   Write odd or even at the end.

   a 16 =  = _____

   b 13 =  = _____

5. Answer these. Use drawings if it helps.

    a 15 − 4 = _____

    b 18 − 6 = _____

6. Answer these. Remember there's an easy way!

    a 23 + 9 = _____

    b 56 − 9 = _____

    c 38 + 9 = _____

    d 41 − 9 = _____

7. Answer these questions.

    a 2×10 = _____   **b** 7×10 = _____

    c 3×10 = _____   **d** 8×10 = _____

8. Would we use cm or m to measure …

    a a flower? _____   **b** a lorry? _____

    c a playground? _____   **d** a pen? _____

9. Cut these shapes in $\frac{1}{2}$.

    a

    b

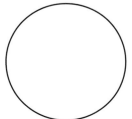

Total

/26

More practice? Go to

More than, less than

63	64	65	66	67	68	69	70	71	72	73	74	75	76	77	78	79	80	81	82	83	84	85	86	87	88

Numbers go up in **order**.

1. **Use the number line.**

   a What is 1 more than 72? __73__

   b What is 1 more than 79? _____

   c What is 1 less than 67? _____

   d What is 1 less than 83? _____

2. **Answer these questions without using a number line.**

   a What is 1 more than 16? _____

   b What is 1 less than 89? _____

   c What is 1 more than 23? _____

   d What is 1 less than 99? _____

3. **Answer these questions. Use this number line.**

   Watch out, it doesn't show every number!

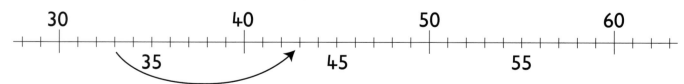

   a What is 10 more than 33? __43__

   b What is 10 more than 41? _____

   c What is 10 less than 45? _____

4. **Answer these questions.**

   a What is 10 less than 62? _____   **b** What is 10 more than 26? _____

   c What is 10 less than 85? _____   **d** What is 10 more than 47? _____

5. **Finish these number patterns.**

a

3	13	23	33			63		

b

96	86	76			46			

6. **Fill in the gaps.**

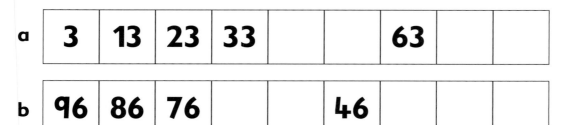

   a 32 →10 more→ _42_   **b** _____ →10 more→ 76

   c 68 →10 more→ _____   **d** _____ →10 more→ 38

How did I do? _____ _____  _____   Total

 18

More practice? Go to www

Challenge yourself

  a I have saved 46p. Aziz has saved 10p more than me.

     How much has Aziz saved? _____

  b Liz has saved 78p. I have saved 10p less than her.

     How much have I saved? _____

Number sentences using 20

There are many different ways of making number sentences using 20. Look at these number sentences…

$$13 + 7 = 20$$

$$20 - 13 = 7$$

The same numbers can be used in addition **and** subtraction number sentences.

1. **Fill in the missing numbers in each pair.**

a _17_ + 3 = 20   20 − 3 = _17_

b 6 + _____ = 20   20 − _____ = 6

c _____ + 9 = 20   20 − _____ = 9

d 12 + _____ = 20   20 − 12 = _____

e _____ + 14 = 20   20 − _____ = 14

f 1 + _____ = 20   20 − _____ = 1

g _____ + 5 = 20   20 − 5 = _____

h 11 + _____ = 20   20 − 11 = _____

i _____ + 13 = 20   20 − 13 = _____

j _____ + 4 = 20   20 − _____ = 4

2. Check these number sentences. ✓ = correct   ✗ = wrong

a 15 + 14 = 20 ☐   **b** 12 + 7 = 20 ☐   **c** 9 + 11 = 20 ☐

d 18 + 3 = 20 ☐   **e** 20 − 17 = 4 ☐   **f** 20 − 5 = 15 ☐

3. Match the cards so that they total 20.   *(8 marks)*

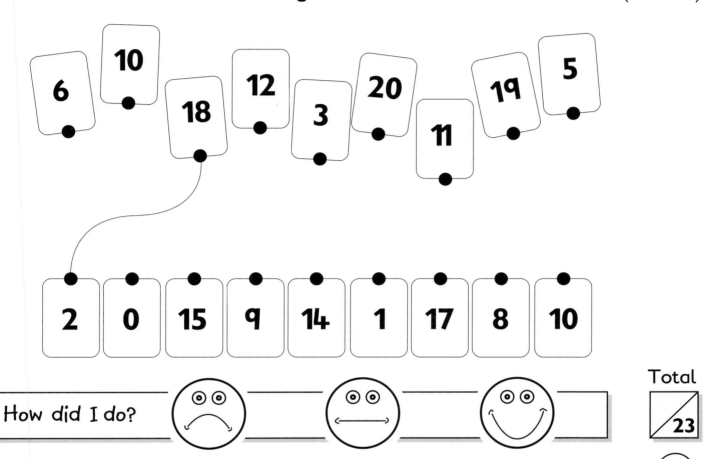

How did I do?

More practice? Go to www

Total ☐ /23

Challenge yourself

Using the same numbers, write a subtraction number sentence.

a 14 + 6 = 20   _20 − 14 = 6 or 20 − 6 = 14_

b 8 + 12 = 20   _____

c 17 + 3 = 20   _____

d 5 + 15 = 20   _____

e 11 + 9 = 20   _____

Adding more than two numbers

We have been adding two numbers together.

$5 + 2 = 7$

We can add **more than two** numbers.

| 6 | + | 5 | + | 2 | = | 13 |

If you are adding more than two numbers, it can help if you write the largest number first.

---

1.   Write the missing numbers. Draw and write the answers.

a

$$\underline{}4 \quad + \quad \underline{}3 \quad + \quad \underline{}3 \quad = \quad \underline{}$$

b

$$\underline{} \quad + \quad \underline{} \quad + \quad \underline{} \quad = \quad \underline{}$$

c

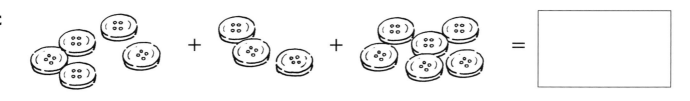

____ + ____ + ____ = ____

2. Add these numbers.

a 7 + 6 + 2 = _____

b 8 + 6 + 5 = _____

c 9 + 9 + 2 = _____

d 10 + 6 + 2 = _____

e 8 + 7 + 3 = _____

How did I do?

Total

/7

More practice? Go to www

Challenge yourself

Find the answer.

a Add 5, 2 and 9. _____

b What is the total of 3, 6 and 7? _____

c Write three numbers that add up to 12. _____ _____ _____

d What is the total of 5, 4 and 7? _____

e Write three numbers that add up to 17. _____ _____ _____

Lesson 13

Add and subtract 11

There is an easy way to **add 11** to a number. $5 + 11 = ?$

Instead of adding 11, **add 10 then add 1**!

$5 + 10 = 15$ then $15 + 1 = 16$ $5 + 11 = 16$

1. **First add 10 to each of these numbers, then add 1.**

a $17 + 10 + 1 =$ _____

b $12 + 10 + 1 =$ _____

c $26 + 10 + 1 =$ _____

d $22 + 10 + 1 =$ _____

2. **Answer these number sentences.**
Use the box to make notes if you need to.

a $13 + 11 =$ _24_

b $19 + 11 =$ _____

c $27 + 11 =$ _____

d $32 + 11 =$ _____

e $54 + 11 =$ _____

f $62 + 11 =$ _____

g $87 + 11 =$ _____

$13 + 10 + 1 = 24$

There is also an easy way to **subtract 11** from a number. $15 - 11 = ?$

Instead of subtracting 11, **subtract 10 then subtract 1**!

$15 - 10 = 5$ then $5 - 1 = 4$ $15 - 11 = 4$

3. **Answer these number sentences.**
Use the box to make notes if you need to.

a 21 − 11 = __10__

b 32 − 11 = _____

c 49 − 11 = _____

d 52 − 11 = _____

e 86 − 11 = _____

f 59 − 11 = _____

g 78 − 11 = _____

$$21 - 10 - 1 = 10$$

How did I do?

Total

16

More practice? Go to www

Challenge yourself

Look carefully at these number sentences.
Add the missing signs to make each one correct.

a 36 [+] 11   is the same as 36 [+] 10 [+] 1 = 47

b 51 [ ] 11   is the same as 51 [ ] 10 [ ] 1 = 40

c 65 [ ] 11   is the same as 65 [ ] 10 [ ] 1 = 54

d 18 [ ] 11   is the same as 18 [ ] 10 [ ] 1 = 29

e 49 [ ] 11   is the same as 49 [ ] 10 [ ] 1 = 60

f 32 [ ] 11   is the same as 32 [ ] 10 [ ] 1 = 21

2 times table

5 lots of 2 is 10 $\circ$ + $\circ$ + $\circ$ + $\circ$ + $\circ$ = 10

         2   2   2   2   2

                     5 × 2   = 10

QUICK TIP!
× means 'lots of' or '**multiply**'

1. **a** $6 \times 2 = \circ + \circ + \circ + \circ + \circ + \circ = $ _____

   b $2 \times 2 = \circ + \circ = $ _____

   c $7 \times 2 = \circ + \circ + \circ + \circ + \circ + \circ + \circ = $ _____

   d $1 \times 2 = \circ = $ _____

   e $9 \times 2 = \circ + \circ + \circ + \circ + \circ + \circ + \circ + \circ + \circ = $ _____

   f $3 \times 2 = \circ + \circ + \circ = $ _____

   g $5 \times 2 = \circ + \circ + \circ + \circ + \circ = $ _____

   h $4 \times 2 = \circ + \circ + \circ + \circ = $ _____

   i $8 \times 2 = \circ + \circ + \circ + \circ + \circ + \circ + \circ + \circ = $ _____

2.

$1 \times 2 =$ _____

$2 \times 2 =$ _____

$3 \times 2 =$ _____

$4 \times 2 =$ _____

$5 \times 2 =$ _____

$6 \times 2 =$ _____

$7 \times 2 =$ _____

$8 \times 2 =$ _____

$9 \times 2 =$ _____

$10 \times 2 =$ _____

3. Fill in the gaps.

a $4 \times 2 =$ ☐

b $3 \times 2 =$ ☐

c ☐ $\times 2 = 2$

d ☐ $\times 2 = 12$

e $8 \times$ ☐ $= 16$

f $5 \times$ ☐ $= 10$

4. Finish the 2 times table number sequences.

a

| 2 | 4 | | 8 | 10 | | 14 | 16 | |

b

| | 4 | | 8 | | 12 | | 16 | |

How did I do?

Total

/27

More practice? Go to **www**

Challenge yourself

Find the answers!

a What is 2 multiplied by 3? _____

b Nine times two is _____ .

c Six children collected 2 conkers each.
How many conkers did they collect altogether? _____

Straight lines

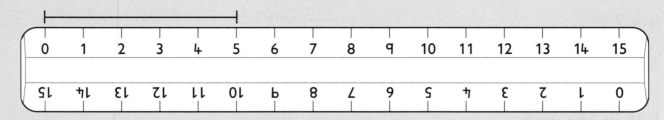

We can draw **straight lines** using a ruler.

Remember we measure **centimetres (cm)** with a ruler.

1. **Draw a line between these dots using a ruler.**

a ●→

b ●→

c ●→

d ●→

e ●→

f ●→ ●

No Nonsense Maths

6-7 years

Parents notes

What your child will learn from this book

Bond No Nonsense will help your child to understand and become more confident in their maths work. This book features all the main maths objectives covered by your child's class teacher during the school year. It provides clear, straightforward teaching and learning of the essentials in a rigorous, step-by-step way.

How you can help

Following a few simple guidelines will ensure that your child gets the best from this book:

- Explain that the book will help your child become confident in their maths work.
- If your child has difficulty reading the text on the page or understanding a question, do provide help.
- Provide scrap paper to give your child extra space for rough working.
- Encourage your child to complete all the exercises in a lesson. You can mark the work using this answer section (which you will also find on the website). Your child can record their own impressions of the work using the 'How did I do' feature.

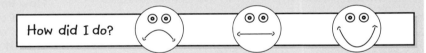

- The 'How am I doing?' sections provide a further review of progress.

Using the website – www.bondlearning.co.uk

- The website provides extra practice of every skill in the book. So if your child does not feel confident about a lesson, they can go to the website and have another go.
- For every page of this book you will find further practice questions and their answers available to download.
- To access the extra practice pages:
  1. Go to www.bondlearning.co.uk
  2. Click on 'Maths'.
  3. Click on '6-7 years'.
  4. Click on the lesson you want.

Bond No Nonsense 6-7 years Answers

(1) Read and write numbers to 100 pp2–3
1. b

c

2. a 72   **b** 45   **c** 58
3. a 5 tens and 3 units   **b** 2 tens and 8 units
   c 9 tens and 7 units   **d** 3 tens and 6 units

Challenge yourself
a fifty-three   **b** forty-nine   **c** eighty-one   **d** 26   **e** 93
f 55   **g** 86

(2) Order and count numbers to 100 pp4–5
1. a   **b**   **c**   **d**

2. a 64   **b** 48   **c** 87   **d** 19, 21   **e** 29, 31
3. a 45   **b** 21   **c** 73   **d** 11   **e** 29   **f** 46
4. a 28   **b** 22   **c** 57   **d** 77   **e** 32   **f** 55

Challenge yourself
b 39 or 40   **c** 20, 21, 22 or 23   **d** 30, 31 or 32
e 32   **f** 69, 70 or 71   **g** 98   **h** 78, 79, 80 or 81

(3) Tens and units pp6–7
1. a 6 tens and 3 units   **b** 2 tens and 8 units
   c 5 tens and 1 unit
2. b 4 tens and 8 units   **c** 5 tens and 7 units
   d 8 tens and 9 units
3. 47 four tens and seven units   72 seven tens and two units
   65 six tens and five units   93 nine tens and three units
   22 two tens and two units   59 five tens and nine units

Challenge yourself
a 90   **b** 3   **c** 17   **d** 6   **e** 30   **f** 42

(4) Odd and even numbers pp8–9
1. b odd   **c** odd
2. b 8   8   even   **c** 10   11   odd
   d 14   14   even   **e** 12   13   odd

Challenge yourself
a / b

| 9 | 10 | 11 | 12 | 13 | 14 | 15 | 16 | 17 | 18 | 19 | 20 | 21 | 22 | 23 | 24 | 25 | 26 | 27 | 28 |

☐ odd   ☐ even

(5) Subtraction 1 pp10–11
1. a 7   **b** 11 − 7 = 4   **c** 17 − 6 = 11   **d** 13 − 8 = 5
   e 17 − 4 = 13
2. a 7   **b** 10   **c** 12   **d** 9
3. a 1   **b** 20   **c** 8   **d** 10
4. a 14   **b** 23   **c** 19   **d** 26   **e** 15
The numbers stay the same.

Challenge yourself
a 6p   **b** 12p   **c** 16p   **d** 6p   **e** 16p   **f** 23p

(6) Add and subtract 9 pp12–13
1. a 18   **b** 22   **c** 31   **d** 36   **e** 25   **f** 13
2. b 26   **c** 43   **d** 31   **e** 85   **f** 68   **g** 90

3. b 28   **c** 20   **d** 58   **e** 73   **f** 32   **g** 81
Challenge yourself
b +   +   −   **c** −   −   +   **d** −   −   +
e +   +   −   **f** −   −   +

(7) 10 times table pp14–15
1. b 30   **c** 70   **d** 40   **e** 10
2. 10   20   30   40   50   60   70   80   90   100
3. a 60   **b** 80   **c** 3   **d** 5   **e** 10   **f** 10
4. a 30   50   70   90   **b** 20   40   50   60

Challenge yourself
a 60   **b** 40   **c** 30

(8) Measuring in centimetres and metres pp16–17
1. b 6 cm   **c** 12 cm   **d** 8 cm   **e** 13½ cm   **f** 3 cm
2. a 100 cm   **b** m   **c** m

Challenge yourself
a cm   **b** cm   **c** m   **d** cm   **e** m   **f** cm

(9) Fractions – a half pp18–19
1. a 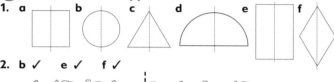   **b**   **c**   **d**   **e**   **f**

2. b ✓   **e** ✓   **f** ✓
3. a

b

c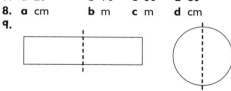

Challenge yourself
a 4   **b** 7   **c** 6   **d** 9   **e** 3   **f** 10

How am I doing? pp20–21
1. a 6 tens and 7 units   **b** 2 tens and 9 units
   c 3 tens and 6 units   **d** 4 tens and 2 units
2. a 31   34   **b** 73   75
3. a 33   **b** 87
4. a even   **b** odd
5. a 11   **b** 12
6. a 32   **b** 47   **c** 47   **d** 32
7. a 20   **b** 70   **c** 30   **d** 80
8. a cm   **b** m   **c** m   **d** cm
9.

(10) More than, less than pp22–23
1. b 80   **c** 66   **d** 82
2. a 17   **b** 88   **c** 24   **d** 98
3. b 51   **c** 35
4. a 52   **b** 36   **c** 75   **d** 57
5. a 43   53   73   83   **b** 66   56   36   26   16
6. b 66   **c** 78   **d** 28

Challenge yourself
a 56p   **b** 68p

(11) Number sentences using 20 pp24–25
1. b 14   **c** 11   **d** 8   **e** 6   **f** 19   **g** 15   **h** 9   **i** 7
   j 16

2. a ✗ **b** ✗ **c** ✓ **d** ✗ **e** ✗ **f** ✓
3. 6 14   10 10   18 2   12 8
     3 17   20 0   11 9   19 1
     5 15

Challenge yourself
b 20 − 8 = 12 or 20 − 12 = 8
c 20 − 17 = 3 or 20 − 3 = 17
d 20 − 5 = 15 or 20 − 15 = 5
e 20 − 11 = 9 or 20 − 9 = 11

⑫ **Adding more than two numbers pp26–27**
1. b 6 + 4 + 5 = 15   **c** 5 + 3 + 6 = 14
2. a 15 **b** 19 **c** 20 **d** 18 **e** 18

Challenge yourself
a 16 **b** 16 **c** Answers will vary
d 16 **e** Answers will vary

⑬ **Add and subtract 11 pp28–29**
1. a 28 **b** 23 **c** 37 **d** 33
2. b 30 **c** 38 **d** 43 **e** 65 **f** 73 **g** 98
3. b 21 **c** 38 **d** 41 **e** 75 **f** 48 **g** 67

Challenge yourself
b − − −   **c** − − −   **d** + + +
e + + +   **f** − − −

⑭ **2 times table pp30–31**
1. a 12 **b** 4 **c** 14 **d** 2 **e** 18 **f** 6 **g** 10
  h 8 **i** 16
2. 2 4 6 8 10 12 14 16 18 20
3. a 8 **b** 6 **c** 1 **d** 6 **e** 2 **f** 2
4. a 6 12 18 **b** 2 6 10 14 18

Challenge yourself
a 6 **b** 18 **c** 12

⑮ **Straight lines pp32–33**
2. a 10 cm **b** 13 cm **c** 7 cm **d** 2 cm **e** 7 cm

Challenge yourself
a 8 cm **b** 12 cm **c** 4 cm **d** 14 cm **e** 7 cm **f** 1 cm

⑯ **Fractions – a quarter pp34–35**
1. a 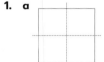 **b**   **c**   **d**

2. a ✓ **c** ✓
3. a

b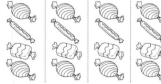

c

d

Challenge yourself
a 3 **b** 4 **c** 1 **d** 5

⑰ **Time – o'clock and half past pp36–37**
1. a 8 o'clock **b** half past 10 **c** 3 o'clock
  d half past 7 **e** half past 1 **f** 11 o'clock
2. a **b** **c** **d**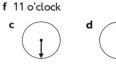

  e **f**

3. a half past 7 **b** 6 o'clock

Challenge yourself
a 4 o'clock **b** half past 3 **c** half past 4

⑱ **Solving problems pp38–39**
1. Answers will vary. Children may decide to use each number and symbol only once in each calculation, or to omit some numbers or symbols from some (or all) calculations.
2.

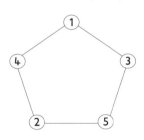

3. Answers will vary.

Challenge yourself
a 1 (6 + 6)
b 6 (1 + 5 + 6, 2 + 4 + 6, 2 + 5 + 5, 3 + 3 + 6, 3 + 4 + 5, 4 + 4 + 4)

How am I doing? pp40–41
1. a 67 **b** 13 **c** 76 **d** 11
2. a 13 **b** 5
3. a 16 **b** 17
4. a 23 **b** 59
5. a 6 **b** 16 **c** 12 **d** 18
6. a 8 cm **b** 13 cm **c** 3 cm
7. a **b**

8. a half past 7 **b** half past 1 **c** half past 4
9. 11 ways:
  10p
  5p + 5p
  5p + 2p + 2p + 1p
  5p + 2p + 1p + 1p +1p
  5p + 1p + 1p +1p + 1p + 1p
  2p + 2p + 2p + 2p + 2p
  2p + 2p + 2p + 2p + 1p + 1p
  2p + 2p + 2p + 1p + 1p + 1p + 1p
  2p + 2p + 1p + 1p + 1p + 1p + 1p + 1p
  2p + 1p + 1p + 1p + 1p + 1p + 1p + 1p + 1p
  1p + 1p + 1p + 1p + 1p + 1p + 1p + 1p + 1p + 1p

⑲ **More than, less than, in between pp42–43**
1. a 32 **b** 30 **c** 44 **d** 78
2. b 25 **c** 37 **d** 37
3. a 39 **b** 39 **c** 38 **d** 40
4. a 36 **b** 68 **c** 24 **d** 11
5. a 72 **b** 28 **c** 55 **d** 87
6. a 58 59 **b** 79 80 **c** 29 30 **d** 17 18 **e** 51 52
  f 92 93
7. a 15 **b** 25

Challenge yourself
a 20p   **b** 29 cm   **c** 12p

⟨20⟩ Counting in steps pp44–45
1. **a** 3   **b** 2   **b** 4

2. **a**

3. **a** 20   24   28   **b** 20   25   30   35
   c 8   10   12   14   **d** 12   15   18   21
4. (3), (6), 9, 12, 15, 18, 21, 24 should be coloured blue.
   The coloured numbers are in two columns.

Challenge yourself
a 8   12   20   **b** 3   9   15   **c** 4   6   10   12

⟨21⟩ Number sequences pp46–47
1. **a** The numbers go up 3 each time.
   b The numbers go down 5 each time.
   c The numbers go up 2 each time.
   d The numbers go down 6 each time.
2. **a** 16   14   12   10   8
   b 10   13   16   19   22
   c 25   31   37   43   49
   d 20   16   12   8   4
3. 24   27

Challenge yourself
Answers will vary

⟨22⟩ Rounding to the nearest 10 pp48–49
1. **b** 20   **c** 10   **d** 20   **e** 30   **f** 20   **g** 10
2. **a** 10   **b** 20   **c** 10   **d** 20   **e** 30   **f** 20   **g** 20

Challenge yourself
a 10   **b** 20

⟨23⟩ Subtraction 2 pp50–51
1. **a** 14   **b** 3   **c** 10   **d** 9   **e** 14   **f** 28   **g** 17
   h 33
2. **a** 5   **b** 10   **c** 7   **d** 6   **e** 27   **f** 15   **g** 6
   h 3
3. **a** 11   **b** 6   **c** 27   **d** 17   **e** 6   **f** 7   **g** 4

Challenge yourself
a 33
b 21

⟨24⟩ 5 times table pp52–53
1. **a** 30   **b** 45   **c** 10   **d** 25   **e** 50   **f** 5   **g** 35
   h 20
2. 5   10   15   20   25   30   35   40   45   50
3. **a** 30   **b** 6   **c** 10   **d** 5   **e** 8   **f** 3
4. **a** 15   20   30   40   45   **b** 5   15   25   30   40   50

Challenge yourself
a 30   **b** 40   **c** 20

⟨25⟩ Division pp54–55
1. **a** 4   **b** 4
2. **b** 3   **c** 2   **d** 4

Challenge yourself
3 each

⟨26⟩ Division facts pp56–57
1. **b** $2 \times 2 = 4$ $4 \div 2 = 2$
   c $3 \times 2 = 6$ $6 \div 2 = 3$
   d $4 \times 2 = 8$ $8 \div 2 = 4$
   e $5 \times 2 = 10$ $10 \div 2 = 5$
   f $6 \times 2 = 12$ $12 \div 2 = 6$
   g $7 \times 2 = 14$ $14 \div 2 = 7$
   h $8 \times 2 = 16$ $16 \div 2 = 8$
   i $9 \times 2 = 18$ $18 \div 2 = 9$
   j $10 \times 2 = 20$ $20 \div 2 = 10$
2. **a** 4   **b** 20   **c** 3   **d** 14   **e** 5   **f** 10   **g** 8   **h** 16

Challenge yourself
a 10, 10   **b** 5, 5   **c** 18, 2   **d** 35, 35   **e** 10, 6   **f** 5, 45

⟨27⟩ Money pp58–59
1. **b** 5p 2p   **c** 10p 5p   **d** 10p 1p
   e 5p 2p 1p   **f** 10p 2p 1p
2. **b** 50p 10p   **c** 20p 5p   **d** 50p 5p
   e 20p 1p   **f** 20p 10p 2p

Challenge yourself
a 4p
b 13p
c £14

⟨28⟩ Time – quarter to and quarter past pp60–61
1. **b** quarter past 4
   c quarter past 10
   d quarter past 1
2. **b** quarter to 5
   c quarter to 12
   d quarter to 3
3. **a**   **b**   **c**   **d**

Challenge yourself
a quarter past 3   **b** 4   **c** quarter to 5

How am I doing? pp62–63
1. **a** 72   **b** 54
2. **a** 12   15   18   **b** 15   17   19
3. The numbers go down by 4 each time.
4. **a** 20   **b** 30
5. **a** 8   **b** 16   **c** 6   **d** 17
6. **a** 25   **b** 35   **c** 15   **d** 45
7. 3
8. **a** 4   **b** 9
9. 10p   10p   1p
10. **a** quarter to 8   **b** quarter past 7

2. Measure these lines.

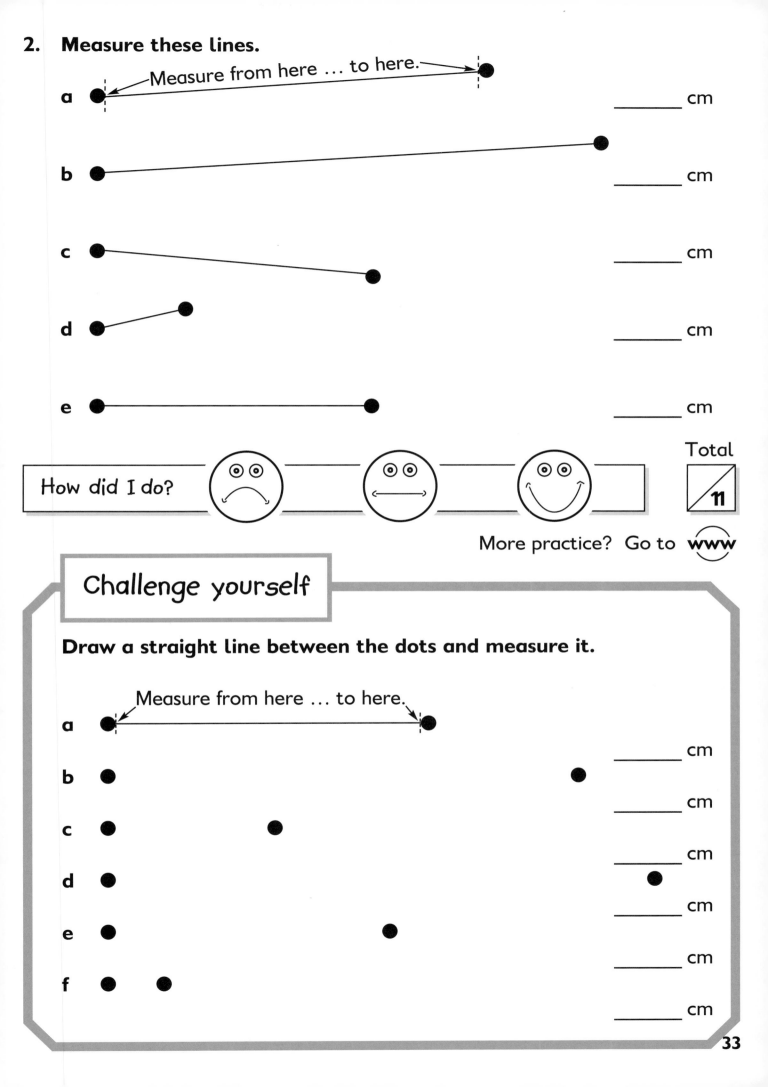

Measure from here ... to here.

a   _____ cm

b   _____ cm

c   _____ cm

d   _____ cm

e   _____ cm

How did I do?   Total

More practice? Go to www

Challenge yourself

Draw a straight line between the dots and measure it.

Measure from here ... to here.

a   _____ cm

b   _____ cm

c   _____ cm

d   _____ cm

e   _____ cm

f   _____ cm

33

Fractions – a quarter

Look at this cake.   If we cut it into four **equal** parts it looks like this.

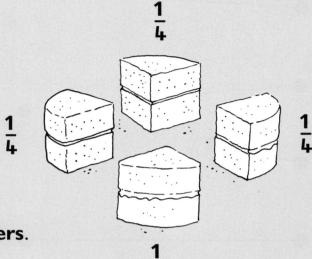

We say we have cut it into **quarters**.

We write a **quarter** like this ... $\frac{1}{4}$

We can cut shapes into quarters.

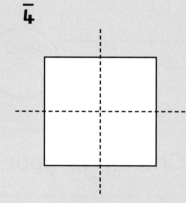

1. Cut these shapes into quarters.

a    b 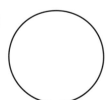   c 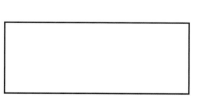   d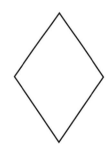

2. Tick the shapes that have been cut into quarters.

a 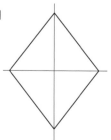   b 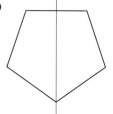   c 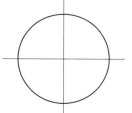   d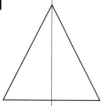

We can work out fractions of a number.

Splitting something into quarters gives four equal parts.

If we split a number into quarters, we do the same. $\frac{1}{4}$ of 8 = 2

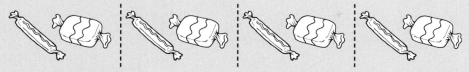

3. **Split these groups of sweets into quarters.**

a 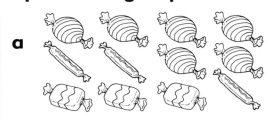   b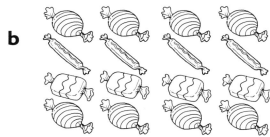

c 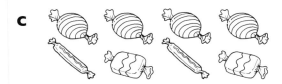   d

How did I do?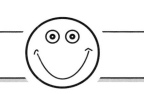

Total

/ 12

More practice? Go to **www**

Challenge yourself

Use drawings to help you if you need to.

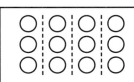

a What is $\frac{1}{4}$ of 12? _____

b What is $\frac{1}{4}$ of 16? _____

c What is $\frac{1}{4}$ of 4? _____

d What is $\frac{1}{4}$ of 20? _____

Time – o'clock and half past

Remember...

This clock shows **5 o'clock**.

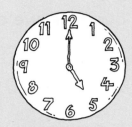

This clock shows **half past 5**.

When the **big hand points to the 6** the time is **half past**.

1. **What time do these clocks show?**

a  _____ o'clock

b  half past _____

c  _____ o'clock

d  half past _____

e  half past _____

f  _____ o'clock

2. **Draw the big hand on these clocks.**

a   9 o'clock

b half past 2

c half past 6

d 10 o'clock

e 4 o'clock

f   half past 1

3.   **What time do these clocks show?**

a _____

b _____

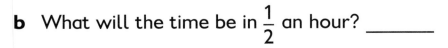

How did I do?

Total

14

More practice? Go to www

Challenge yourself

It is 3 o'clock.

a What will the time be in 1 hour? _____

b What will the time be in $\frac{1}{2}$ an hour? _____

c What will the time be in $1\frac{1}{2}$ hours? _____

37

Solving problems

When you try to solve a problem ...
you are looking for an answer.

Sometimes there is more
than one answer!

1. **How many different answers can you make?**

You can only use these numbers and signs: **2** **5** **6** **+** **–** **=** .
Show your workings.

2. **Place the numbers 1, 2, 3, 4 and 5 in the circles.**
The difference between two joined numbers must
be more than 1.

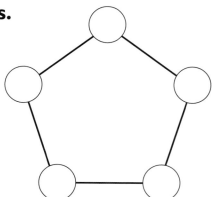

3. **Gary has 25p in his pocket.**

What coins might he have in his pocket?
There is more than one answer to this question!

How did I do?

Total

3

More practice? Go to **www**

Challenge yourself

a How many different ways can you score 12
when you throw two dice?

_____

b How many different ways can you score 12
when you throw three dice?

_____

39

1. **a** What is 10 more than 57? _____

b What is 10 less than 23? _____

c What is 10 less than 86? _____

d What is 10 more than 1? _____

2. **Fill in the gaps.**

a   7 + ☐ = 20   20 – 7 = ☐

b ☐ + 15 = 20   20 – ☐ = 15

3. **a** Add 5, 8 and 3. _____

b Add 6, 9 and 2. _____

4. **Answer these. Remember there's an easy way!**

a 34 – 11 = _____   **b** 48 + 11 = _____

5. **a** $3 \times 2 =$ _____   **b** $8 \times 2 =$ _____

c $6 \times 2 =$ _____   **d** $9 \times 2 =$ _____

6. **Draw a straight line between the dots and measure it with a ruler.**

Measure from here ... to here.

a ●   ● _____ cm

b ●   ● _____ cm

c ●   ● _____ cm

7. **Cut these shapes into quarters.**

a

b

8. **What is the time?**

a half past _____ **b** half past _____ **c** half past _____

9. **Dan buys some sweets. He is given 10p change.**

How many different ways can he be given his change? _____

Use this box for your workings.

More than, less than, in between

Do you remember? ... Numbers go up in order.

25	26	27	28	29	30	31	32	33	34	35	36	37	38	39	40	41	42	43	44

The number line will help!

1. **a** What is 1 more than 31? _____

    b What is 10 less than 40? _____

    c What is 10 more than 34? _____

    d What is 1 less than 79? _____

2. **Which is less?**

    a 28 or 25? _25___   **b** 25 or 35? _____

    c 44 or 37? _____   **d** 37 or 38? _____

3. **Which is more?**

    a 30 or 39? _____   **b** 39 or 29? _____

    c 37 or 38? _____   **d** 40 or 39? _____

Now try these without using a number line.

4. **Which is less?**

    a 36 or 63? _____   **b** 68 or 86? _____

    c 24 or 42? _____   **d** 11 or 19? _____

5. **Which is more?**

    a 38 or 72? _____   **b** 28 or 18? _____

    c 44 or 55? _____   **d** 87 or 78? _____

Look at the numbers 64 and 69. Four numbers lie between them.

| 56 | 57 | 58 | 59 | 60 | 61 | 62 | 63 | 64 | 65 | 66 | 67 | 68 | 69 | 70 | 71 | 72 | 73 | 74 | 75 |

These are 65, 66, 67, 68.

6. Write the two numbers that lie between ...

a 57 _____ _____ 60   **b** 78 _____ _____ 81

c 28 _____ _____ 31   **d** 16 _____ _____ 19

e 50 _____ _____ 53   **f** 91 _____ _____ 94

7.

```
10          ↑          20                    30
```

a Which number is halfway between 10 and 20? _____

b Which number is halfway between 20 and 30? _____

How did I do?

Total
/27

More practice? Go to **www**

Challenge yourself

Answer these questions.

a A bun cost 1p more than 19p and 1p less than 21p.
How much did it cost? _____

b A piece of string is 2 cm longer than 27 cm and 2 cm shorter than 31 cm.
How long is it? _____

c Some sweets cost halfway between 10p and 14p.
What did they cost? _____

43

Counting in steps

Look at the frog. It is jumping along a number line.

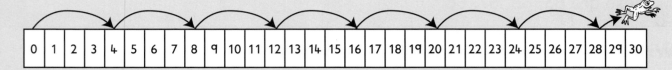

The frog jumps up 4 numbers each time.

1. **How many numbers does the frog jump up each time?**

a

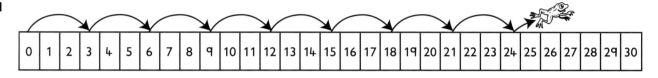

_____ numbers each time.

b

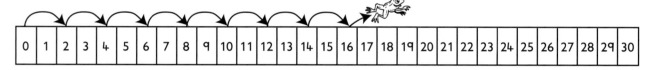

_____ numbers each time.

c

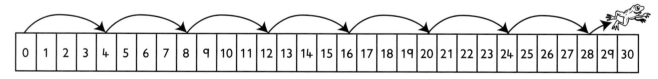

_____ numbers each time.

2. **Finish the jumps, keeping them the same.**

a

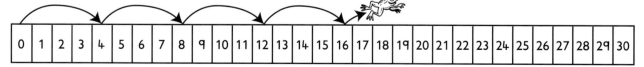

b

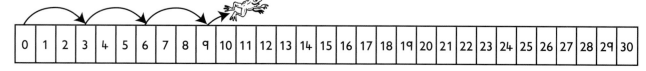

44

3. **Which numbers come next?**

Make sure the numbers go up by the same amount each time.

a | 4 | 8 | 12 | 16 | | | |

b | 5 | 10 | 15 | | | | |

c | 2 | 4 | 6 | | | | |

d | 3 | 6 | 9 | | | | |

4. **Colour blue the numbers that go up by 3 each time.**

What do you notice?

_____

_____

_____

1	2	3	4	5	6
7	8	9	10	11	12
13	14	15	16	17	18
19	20	21	22	23	24

How did I do? _____ _____  _____

Total

/10

More practice? Go to

Challenge yourself

Fill in the missing numbers.

a   4   [ ]   [ ]   16   [ ]   24

b   [ ]   6   [ ]   12   [ ]   18

c   2   [ ]   [ ]   8   [ ]   [ ]

Number sequences

This is a number sequence.

5	10	15	20	25	30

Rule – the numbers go up **5** each time.

The **rule** tells us what happens to the numbers in the number sequence.

1. **Write a rule for each number sequence.**

a

9	12	15	18	21	24

Rule –_____

b

40	35	30	25	20	15

Rule –_____

c

19	21	23	25	27	29

Rule –_____

d

36	30	24	18	12	6

Rule –_____

2. Finish the number sequence to match each rule.

a Rule – the numbers go down 2 each time.

18					

b Rule – the numbers go up 3 each time.

7					

c Rule – the numbers go up 6 each time.

19					

d Rule – the numbers go down 4 each time.

24					

3. **Look at this number sequence and the rule.**
Rule – the numbers go down 3 each time.
Two numbers have been swapped over.
Put a circle around them.

42	39	36	33	30	24	27	21	18	15

How did I do?   ☹   😐   ☺

Total

9

More practice? Go to www

Challenge yourself

**Make your own number pattern and write a rule for it.
It must have the numbers 10 and 15 in it!**

Rule –_____

Rounding to the nearest 10

Look at the number line.

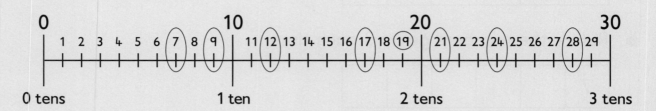

19 is closer to the number 20 than the number 10.

1. **Look at the number line.**

a Is 9 closer to the number 0 or 10? _10_

b Is 17 closer to the number 10 or 20? _____

c Is 12 closer to the number 10 or 20? _____

d Is 24 closer to the number 20 or 30? _____

e Is 28 closer to the number 20 or 30? _____

f Is 21 closer to the number 20 or 30? _____

g Is 7 closer to the number 10 or 20? _____

We can also say **the nearest ten to 19 is 20**.

49

2. **Look at the number line and fill in the gaps.**

a The nearest ten to 13 is _____ .

b The nearest ten to 21 is _____ .

c The nearest ten to 7 is _____ .

d The nearest ten to 18 is _____ .

e The nearest ten to 28 is _____ .

f The nearest ten to 16 is _____ .

g The nearest ten to 24 is _____ .

Total

How did I do?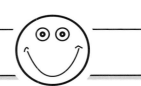

/13

More practice? Go to www

Challenge yourself

Deano ran in a race. He took 9 seconds.
Tim took 17 seconds.
Pen took 12 seconds.

a Deano and Pen each took about _____ seconds, rounded to the nearest ten.

b Tim took about _____ seconds, rounded to the nearest ten.

49

Subtraction 2

Remember ... – means '**subtract**', '**find the difference between**' or '**take away**'.

15   –   7   =   8

1. **Write the answers. Use the number line below to help you.**

    a 20 – 6 = _____   **b** 9 – 6 = _____

    c 17 – 7 = _____   **d** 18 – 9 = _____

    e 22 – 8 = _____   **f** 35 – 7 = _____

    g 27 – 10 = _____   **h** 39 – 6 = _____

2. **Fill in the gaps.**

    a 17 – ☐ = 12   **b** 18 – ☐ = 8

    c 12 – 5 = ☐   **d** 20 – ☐ = 14

    e ☐ – 6 = 21   **f** ☐ – 5 = 10

    g 14 – 8 = ☐   **h** 17 – ☐ = 14

Here is a number line to help you.

1	2	3	4	5	6	7	8	9	10	11	12	13	14	15	16	17	18	19	20

3. **Find the answers. Remember to use the number line if you need to.**

   a   17 take away 6. _____

   b   Take 14 from 20. _____

   c   35 subtract 8. _____

   d   Subtract 5 from 22. _____

   e   What is the difference between 17 and 23? _____

   f   What must I add to 12 to make 19? _____

   g   33 add a number is 37. What is the number? _____

How did I do?   🙁 — 😐 — 🙂

Total ⬛/**23**

More practice? Go to www

Challenge yourself

I had 40 sweets in a bag. I ate 7.

   a   How many sweets did
         I have left? _____

   b   Then I ate 12 more! How many sweets do I have left now? _____

| 21 | 22 | 23 | 24 | 25 | 26 | 27 | 28 | 29 | 30 | 31 | 32 | 33 | 34 | 35 | 36 | 37 | 38 | 39 | 40 |

5 times table

3 lots of 5 is 15

$3 \times 5 = 15$

QUICK TIP!
x means 'lots of' or 'multiply'

1. **a** $6 \times 5 =$ 　　　　　　　　　　　　　 = _____

b $9 \times 5 =$ 　　　　　　　　　　　　　 = _____

c $2 \times 5 =$ 　　　　 = _____

d $5 \times 5 =$ 　　　　　　　　 = _____

e $10 \times 5 =$ 　　　　　　　　　　　 = _____

f $1 \times 5 =$ 　　 = _____

g $7 \times 5 =$ 　　　　　　　　　 = _____

h $4 \times 5 =$ 　　　　　　 = _____

2.

$1 \times 5 =$ _____ $5 \times 5 =$ _____ $9 \times 5 =$ _____

$2 \times 5 =$ _____ $6 \times 5 =$ _____ $10 \times 5 =$ _____

$3 \times 5 =$ _____ $7 \times 5 =$ _____

$4 \times 5 =$ _____ $8 \times 5 =$ _____

3. Fill in the gaps.

a $6 \times 5 =$ ☐   **b** ☐ $\times 5 = 30$ **c** $2 \times 5 =$ ☐

d $10 \times$ ☐ $= 50$ **e** ☐ $\times 5 = 40$ **f** ☐ $\times 5 = 15$

4. Finish the 5 times table number sequences.

a

5	10			25		35			50

b

	10		20			35		45	

How did I do?			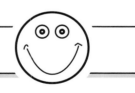	Total /26

More practice? Go to www

Challenge yourself

Find the answer!

a What are six fives? _____

b Multiply 5 by 8. _____

c Sarah bought 4 packets of stickers. There were five stickers in each packet.

How many stickers did she have altogether? _____

Division

Divide 6 sweets **equally** between Emma and Rob.

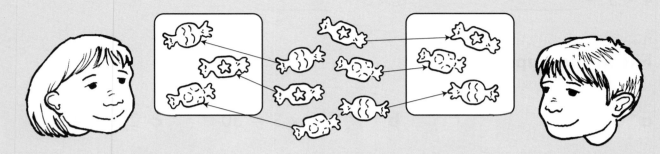

6 sweets shared equally by 2 = 3 each.

1. **a** Share 8 sweets equally between 2 children.

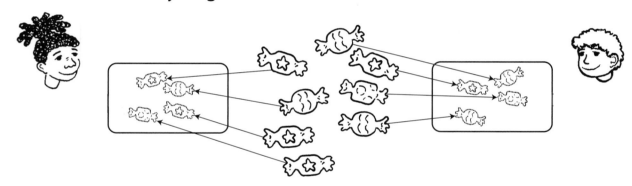

How many do they have each? _____ each.

b Share 12 sweets equally between 3 children.

How many do they have each? _____ each.

If we divide 6 sweets equally between 2 children they get 3 sweets each. We write the number sentence like this

6 ÷ 2 = 3

QUICK TIP!
÷ means 'divide by' or 'shared between'

2. **Answer these questions.**
    Share out the numbers into the boxes if it helps.

a 4 ÷ 2 = _2_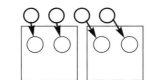

b 9 ÷ 3 = ____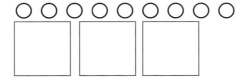

c 10 ÷ 5 = ____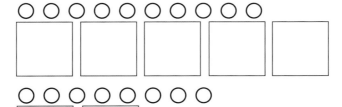

d 8 ÷ 2 = ____

How did I do?   _____  _____

Total
/5

More practice? Go to www

Challenge yourself

Brian had nine sweets. He shared them equally with two of his friends, John and Sean. How many did they each have?

____   ____   ____
Brian   John   Sean

Division facts

In this book we have been learning the 10x, 2x and 5x tables.
Did you know they can help you with division?
Look...

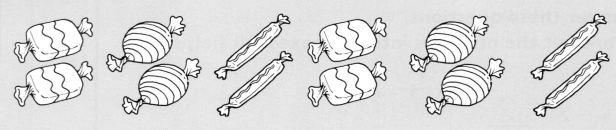

6 x 2 = 12

12 ÷ 6 = 2

1. **Match the multiplication fact to its division fact with a line.**

a	$1 \times 2 = 2$	$16 \div 2 = 8$
b	$2 \times 2 = 4$	$20 \div 2 = 10$
c	$3 \times 2 = 6$	$10 \div 2 = 5$
d	$4 \times 2 = 8$	$4 \div 2 = 2$
e	$5 \times 2 = 10$	$6 \div 2 = 3$
f	$6 \times 2 = 12$	$12 \div 2 = 6$
g	$7 \times 2 = 14$	$8 \div 2 = 4$
h	$8 \times 2 = 16$	$2 \div 2 = 1$
i	$9 \times 2 = 18$	$14 \div 2 = 7$
j	$10 \times 2 = 20$	$18 \div 2 = 9$

2. **Finish the multiplication or division fact.**
This time we will also use some facts from the 10x table.

a 4 × 2 = 8   8 ÷ 2 = ☐

b 20 ÷ 2 = 10   10 × 2 = ☐

c 3 × 10 = 30   30 ÷ 10 = ☐

d 14 ÷ 2 = 7   7 × 2 = ☐

e 5 × 10 = 50   50 ÷ 10 = ☐

f 10 ÷ 2 = 5   5 × 2 = ☐

g 8 × 10 = 80   80 ÷ 10 = ☐

h 16 ÷ 2 = 8   8 × 2 = ☐

Total

| How did I do? |  |  | | /17 |

More practice? Go to

Challenge yourself

Add the missing numbers to the boxes.

a   10 × ☐ = 100   100 ÷ ☐ = 10

b   25 ÷ 5 = ☐   ☐ × 5 = 25

c   ☐ ÷ 2 = 9   9 × ☐ = 18

d   7 × 5 = ☐   ☐ ÷ 5 = 7

e   60 ÷ ☐ = 6   10 × ☐ = 60

f   9 × ☐ = 45   ☐ ÷ 5 = 9

57

Money

Look at these coins ...

1. **Draw the coins that need to be added together to make each total. Use the smallest number of coins you can.**

a 6p

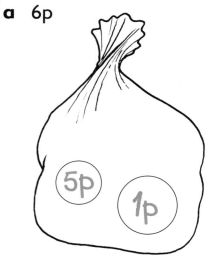

b 7p

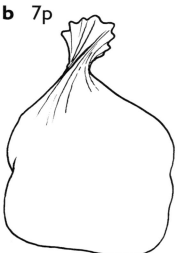

c 15p

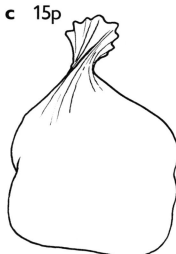

d 11p

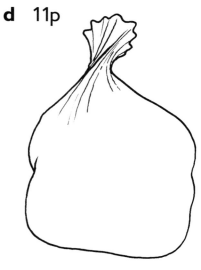

e 8p

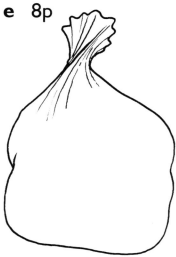

f 13p

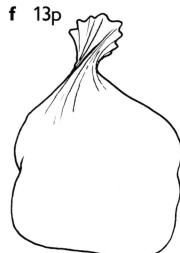

Here are two more coins we use.

2. **Now write which coins you would use to make each total.**
Use the smallest number of coins you can.

a 72p = _50_ p + _20_ p + _2_ p

b 60p = _____ p + _____ p

c 25p = _____ p + _____ p

d 55p = _____ p + _____ p

e 21p = _____ p + _____ p

f 32p = _____ p + _____ p + _____ p

Total

| How did I do? | | |  |

/10

More practice? Go to

Challenge yourself

a Anil spent 16p on sweets. What was his change from 20p? _____ p

b Rosie had 25p. She spent 12p. How much did she have left? _____ p

c Tim's Gran gave him £5 and his uncle gave him £9.
How much money did he get altogether? £_____

Time – quarter to and quarter past

This clock shows **quarter past** 2.

When the big hand moves around to the 3, the time is **quarter past**.
The little hand is just past the 2.

1.   What is the time?

a      quarter past 6

b   _____

c   _____

d   _____

This clock shows **quarter to** 2.

When the big hand moves around to the 9, the time is **quarter to**.
The little hand is just before the 2.

2. **What is the time?**

a  __quarter to 8_____

b  _____

c  _____

d  _____

3. **Draw the big hand on the clocks.**

a quarter past 6    b quarter past 3

c quarter to 5   d quarter past 11

Total

How did I do?      /10

More practice? Go to www

Challenge yourself

It is quarter past 4.

a What time was it 1 hour ago? _____

b In how many hours will it be quarter past 8? _____

c What time will it be in half an hour's time? _____

61

How am I doing?

1. Which is more?

    a 68 or 72 _____

    b 54 or 45 _____

2. Which numbers come next?

    a | 3 | 6 | 9 | | | |

    b | 9 | 11 | 13 | | | |

3. Write a rule for this number sequence.

| 36 | 32 | 28 | 24 | 20 | 16 | 12 | 8 |

Rule _____

4. **a** The nearest ten to 18 is _____ .

      b The nearest ten to 32 is _____ .

5. Fill the gaps.

    a $17 - 9 =$ **b** $22 - 6 =$

    c $11 - 5 =$ **d** $26 - 9 =$

6. **Find the answers.**

a $5 \times 5 = \boxed{}$

b $7 \times 5 = \boxed{}$

c $3 \times 5 = \boxed{}$

d $9 \times 5 = \boxed{}$

7. **Equally share the circles into the boxes to help find the answer.**

○ ○ ○ ○ ○ ○ ○ ○ ○

$9 \div 3 = \underline{}$

$\boxed{}$ $\boxed{}$ $\boxed{}$

8. **Finish the multiplication and division facts.**

a $4 \times 10 = 40$

$40 \div 10 = \boxed{}$

b $18 \div 2 = 9$

$\boxed{} \times 2 = 18$

9. **Write the three coins you would need to make 21p.**

$\underline{}$ p $\underline{}$ p $\underline{}$ p

10. **What is the time?**

a

quarter $\underline{}$

b

quarter $\underline{}$

Total

21

More practice? Go to www

Try the 7–8 years book

Addition and subtraction facts

Remember, when you see **+** think '**add**', '**total**' or '**altogether**'.

16 + 4 = 20

Remember, when you see **−** think '**subtract**', '**find the difference between**' or '**take away**'.

20 − 16 = 4

1. **Complete these number sentences.**

    a 13 + 6 = _____   **b** 19 − 8 = _____

    c 17 − 9 = _____   **d** 10 + 9 = _____

    e 12 + 8 = _____   **f** 20 − 7 = _____

    g 19 − 11 = _____   **h** 11 + 8 = _____

2. **Fill in the gaps.**

    a 19 − ☐ = 11   **b** 12 + ☐ = 20

    c 17 + 2 = ☐   **d** 20 − ☐ = 14

    e ☐ − 6 = 13   **f** ☐ + 5 = 17

    g 9 + 8 = ☐   **h** 14 − ☐ = 7